Inside the Puppet Theatre

Contents

Meet Ronnie   2
The puppet theatre   4
All sorts of characters   6
String and rod puppets   8
Glove and shadow puppets   10
Making a puppet   12
How should it move?   14
A new show   16
The show opens   18
Glossary   20
Index   21
Inside the puppet theatre   22

Written by Claire Llewellyn   Photographed by Véronique Leplat

Collins

Meet Ronnie

My name is Ronnie and I'm a **puppeteer**. A puppeteer works with puppets and puts on puppet shows.

I usually work in a puppet theatre, but you see puppets in other places, too – in schools, on television and even by the sea!

puppets by the sea

puppets at school

The puppet theatre

This is the puppet theatre where I work. It's an old place with steep, wooden staircases and tiny rooms.

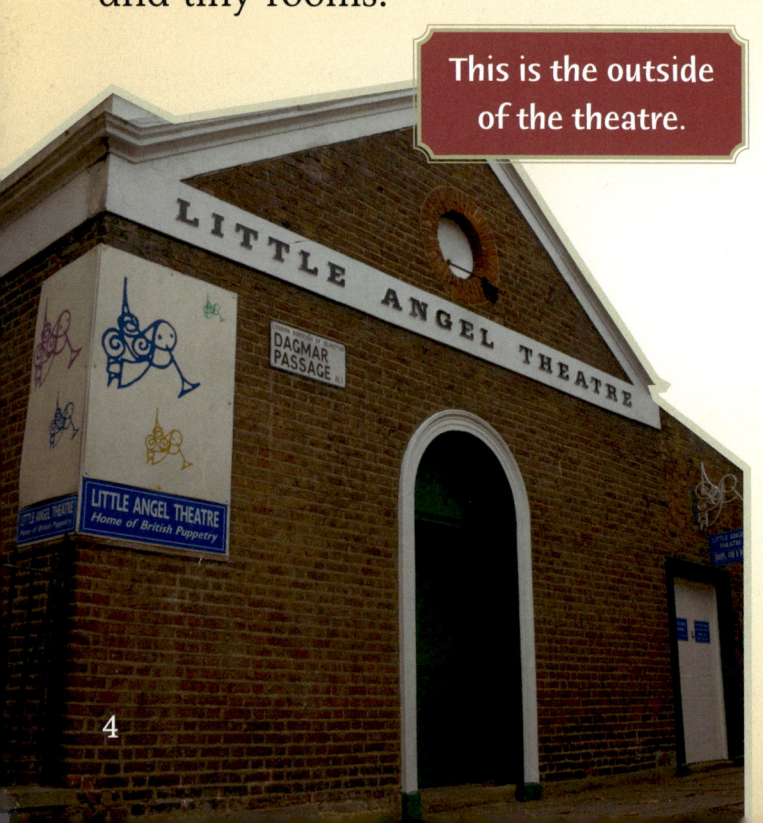

This is the outside of the theatre.

This is the box office where you buy your ticket.

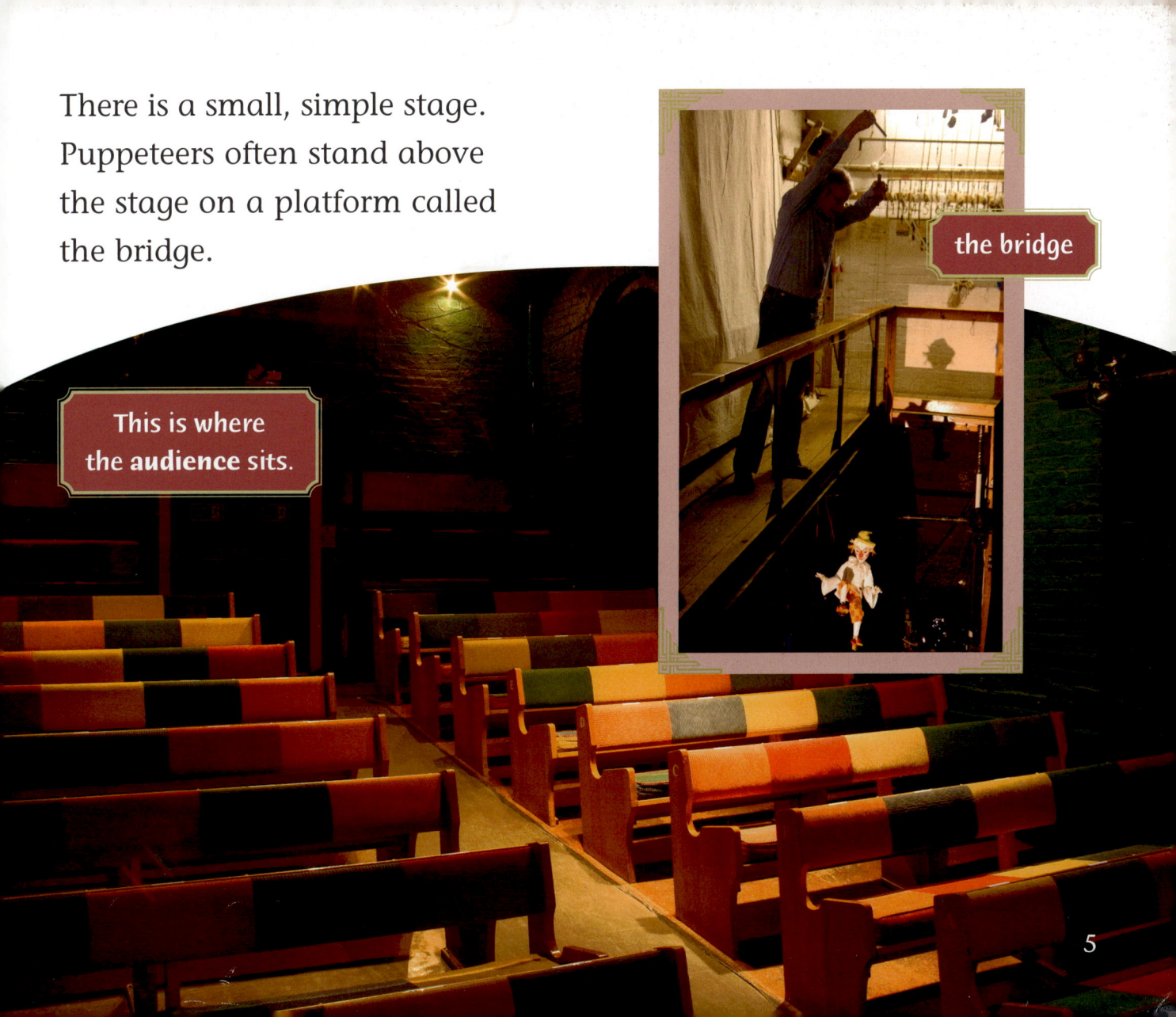

There is a small, simple stage. Puppeteers often stand above the stage on a platform called the bridge.

the bridge

This is where the **audience** sits.

All sorts of characters

There are puppets everywhere. They sit on shelves and hang from rails and lie curled up in boxes.

puppets sitting on a shelf

puppets hanging from rails

Every puppet has a different **character**. There are poor children, kings and wicked stepmothers. There are giants and other make-believe characters. There are monkeys, mice, lizards, giraffes – animals of every kind.

Billy, a boy puppet

a mouse puppet

String and rod puppets

Puppets work in different ways. This is a string puppet. Most of its body is made of wood. There are **joints** at its neck, its elbow and so on. These are the parts of the puppet that move when I pull on the strings.

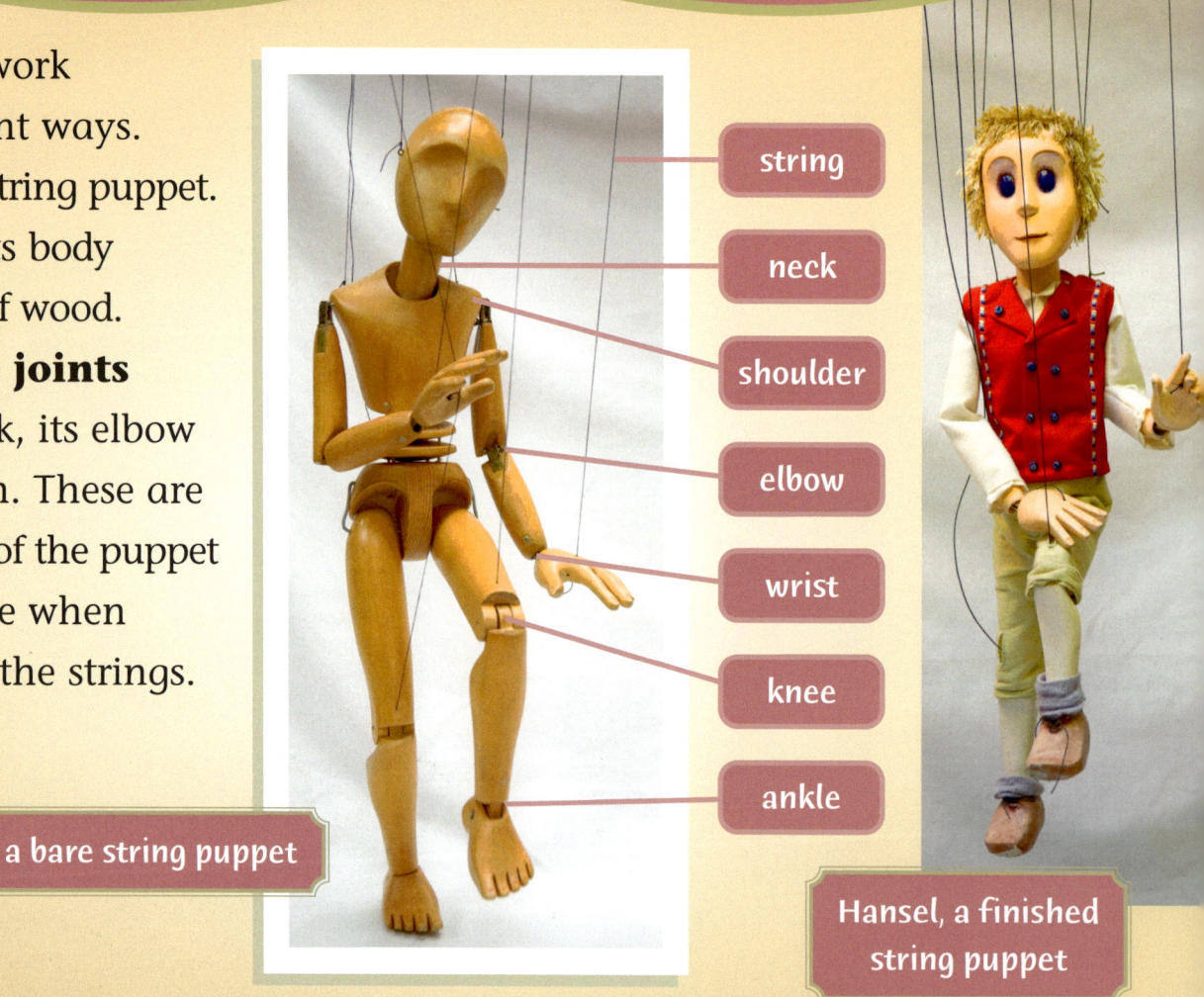

- string
- neck
- shoulder
- elbow
- wrist
- knee
- ankle

a bare string puppet

Hansel, a finished string puppet

8

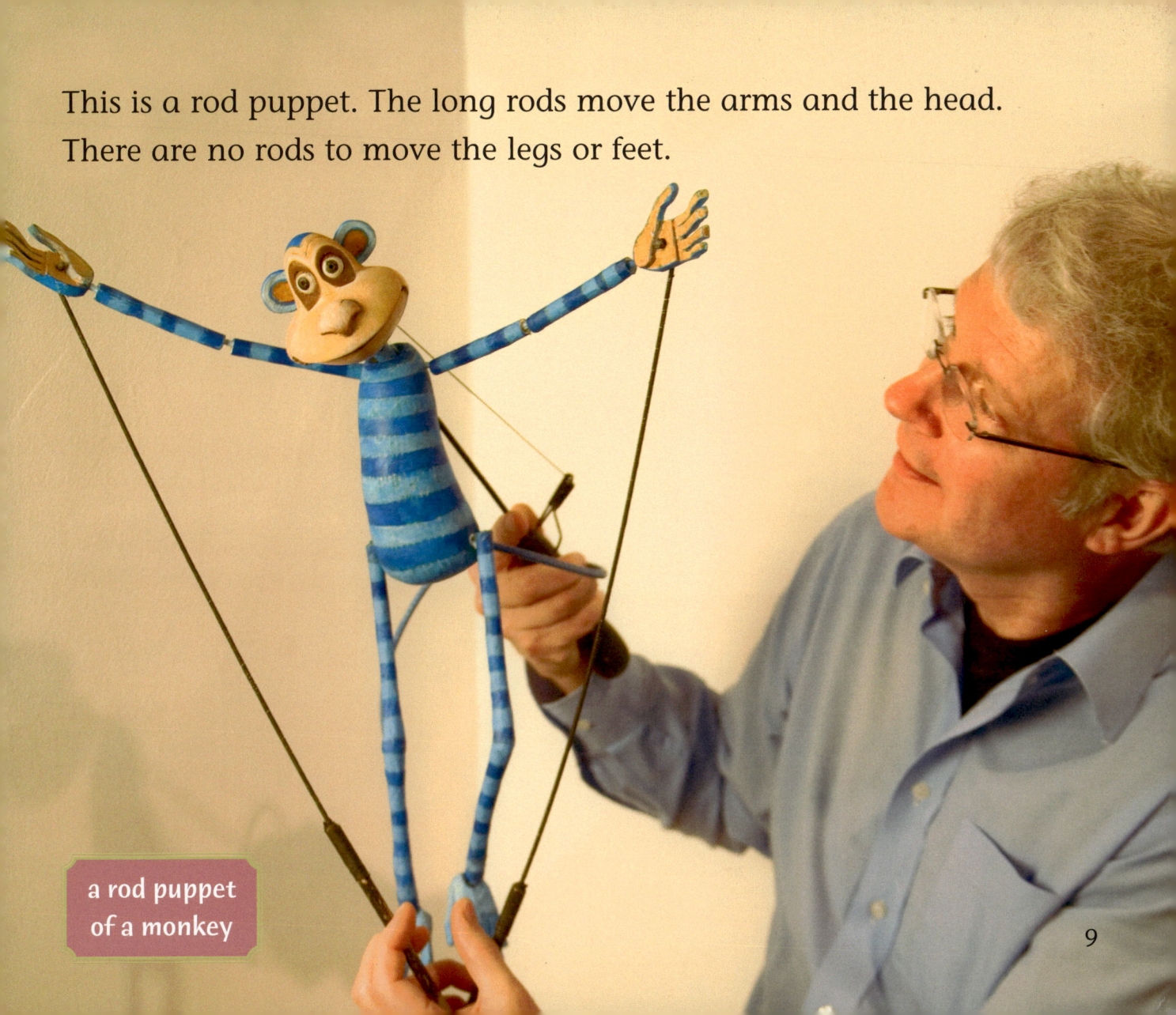

This is a rod puppet. The long rods move the arms and the head. There are no rods to move the legs or feet.

a rod puppet of a monkey

Glove and shadow puppets

This is a glove puppet. You wear it on your hand like a glove and move it with your fingers. Puppets like this get a lot of wear and tear, so they often need repairing.

You hold your hand like this in a glove puppet.

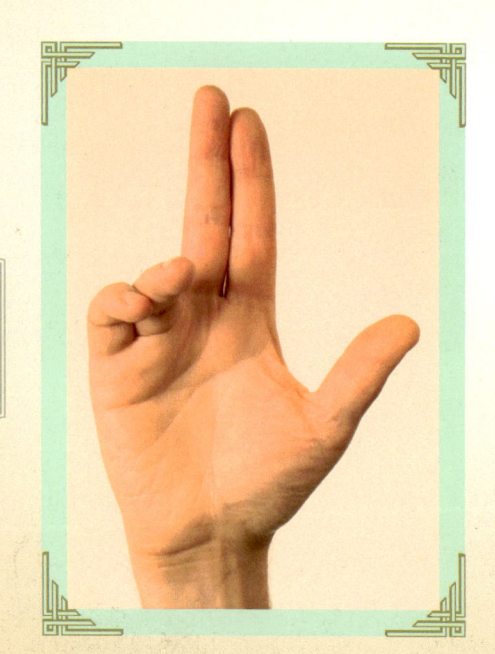

a glove puppet of a wizard

Shadow puppets are different from other puppets. You move them in front of a bright light and make shadows on a screen.

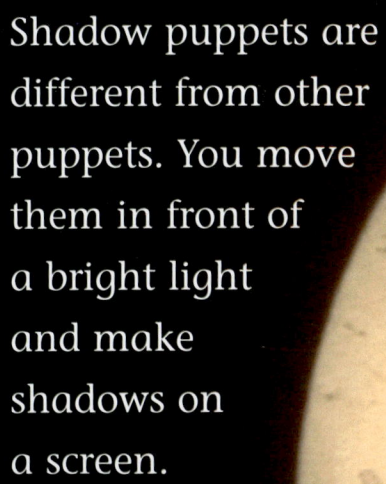

Making a puppet

Every new puppet is made in the workshop. It's a large, light room, crammed with **materials**, paints and tools.

Designers sketch what the puppets should look like. Then a proper drawing is made and the puppet makers get to work.

a designer

the workshop

First, the puppet makers carve each piece of the puppet. Next, they carve and paint its face. Then they make the soft parts of the body and finally the clothes the puppet will wear.

carving the puppet

making the clothes

How should it move?

Whenever I meet a new puppet, I study it, play around with it and see what it can do.

meeting a puppet

I think about the puppet's character and how it should move. Is it young and full of life? Then it will be light on its feet and flit around the stage. Is it large and heavy? Then it will move quite slowly.

fast and light …

… slow and heavy

A new show

Every few months the puppet theatre puts on a new show. A team of people works together.

| The writer thinks about the story and works on the **script**. | The designer plans what the stage and puppets will look like. | Puppet makers begin work on the puppets. |

16

We **rehearse** for a week before the show opens. Everything has to work together – the **set**, the puppets, the lights, the music. Everyone works hard until it all looks and sounds just right.

The puppeteers plan how to move the puppets.

The person in charge is called the **director**.

17

The show opens

About an hour before the show, I change into my black clothes and check that the puppets and **props** are ready. Soon I hear the audience arriving. I can hear children talking and laughing. Then, suddenly, the lights go out. I take a deep breath and start the show.

> I wear black clothes so that you can only see the puppets in the show.

children enjoying the show

19

Glossary

audience   the people who come to see a show

character   the person or animal that a puppet is made to look like

joints   the places where two parts of a puppet's body join and can move

materials   wood, cloth and other things that puppets are made from

props   objects that are used on stage during a show

puppeteer   the person who makes a puppet move

rehearse   to practise a show

script   the words of a play

set   the stage area with the props in place

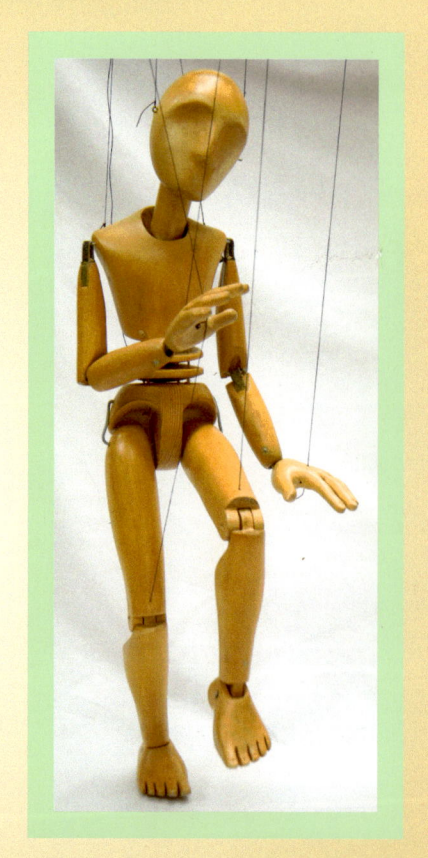

Index

audience 5, 18

designer 12, 16

director 17

glove puppet 10

puppeteer 2, 5, 17

puppet maker 12, 13, 16

puppet show 2, 3, 16, 17, 18

rod puppet 6, 7, 9, 14, 15, 18

theatre 4, 5

stage 5, 15

shadow puppet 11

string puppet 5, 7, 8, 17

writer 16

21

Inside the puppet theatre

box office

stage

workshop

22

bridge

seating

23

Ideas for reading

Written by Clare Dowdall PhD
Lecturer and Primary Literacy Consultant

Learning objectives: draw together ideas and information from across a whole text, using simple signposts in the text; explain organisational features of texts, including alphabetical order, layout, diagrams, captions; work effectively in groups by ensuring that each group member takes a turn challenging, supporting and moving on

Curriculum links: Art: People in action; Design and Technology: Puppets

Interest words: puppeteer, theatre, character, joints, rod, glove, shadow, materials, designers, rehearse, director, props, audience, glossary

Word count: 667

Resources: puppets, whiteboard, ICT

Getting started

- Look at the front cover together and ask children to share their experiences of puppet shows.
- Make a list of the famous puppets that children know, e.g. Punch and Judy, puppets from television programmes.
- Look at the photograph on the front cover. Ask children to discuss the puppet shown, and suggest character features for it. Is it a male or female puppet? Is it good or naughty?
- Read the blurb together. Focus on the word *puppeteer* and help children to read the *eer* ending.
- Turn to the contents. Ask children to read the contents in pairs and select a topic of interest for reading later.

Reading and responding

- Read pp2-3 with the children. Ask children to notice how the text is organised and what features the author uses, e.g. photographs, captions, bold type.
- In pairs, ask children to read the sections of the book that they selected from the contents.
- Ask children, in pairs, to share the key points from their reading. Encourage children to refer to the text and photographs when recounting information.